SPANNING THE THAMES

RICHMOND LOCK

SPANNING THE THAMES

The River and surroundings
from The Barrier to Teddington Lock

Commentary and Stories by
MICHAEL HARRISON

ARTISTS'
CHOICE EDITIONS

First published 2008

Typeset in Stone serif by Charles Hall
Printed in Singapore

ISBN 978-0-9558343-0-1

ARTISTS' CHOICE EDITIONS
Carol Manheim, 31 Ennismore Avenue, London W4 1SE
Dennis Hall, The Foundry, Church Hanborough, Oxford OX29 8AB
email: art.photo@lineone.net

CONTENTS/ILLUSTRATORS

CONTENTS/ILLUSTATORS

Bridges are hands stretched out in greeting, ways of walking on water for those of us with insufficient faith, optimistic and life-accepting. They join communities, break down barriers formed by nature, and are an essential for the game of Pooh Sticks. One of the first acts of an enemy is to bomb them or blow them up.

This book celebrates links across Britain's greatest river but starts with what can be seen as a symbol of our modern defensiveness, the barrier behind which a fearful nation crouches, saying "Go away!" And yet, the Thames Barrier is a thing of beauty, one of the marvels of modern engineering that can take its place alongside the best of the Victorians'.

Flooding has always been a problem in London. Samuel Pepys is constantly using the river as a natural means of transport and those who want to extend their reading should turn to his diaries. On March 20th 1660 he wrote:

> Then to Westminster, where by reason of rain and an Easterly wind, the water was so high that there was boats rowed in King streete and all our yard was drowned, that one could not go to my house, so as no man hath seen the like almost. Most houses full of water.

The barrier was opened officially in May 1984 and was at first closed about twice a year but this has risen sharply and it was closed twice in one month in 2007. With climate change raising sea levels and the wind the existing Thames Barrier is no longer seen as enough protection and plans are already being considered for replacing it, which makes it a good symbol for the way in which nature runs ahead of technology. Our cleverness dooms us.

It is in this part of the river that Conrad's great novel *Heart of Darkness* (1902) begins, with Marlow telling his story while they wait for the tide to turn. Conrad, the foreigner, evokes the magic of this great entry point into London, the great city.

> The sea-reach of the Thames stretched before us like the beginning of an interminable waterway. In the offing the sea and the sky were welded together without a joint, and in the luminous space the tanned sails of the barges drifting up with the tide seemed to stand still in red clusters of canvas sharply peaked, with gleams of varnished sprits. A haze rested on the low shores that ran out to sea in vanishing flatness . . .
>
> The old river in its broad reach rested unruffled at the decline of day, after ages of good service done to the race that peopled its banks, spread out in the tranquil dignity of a waterway leading to the uttermost ends of the earth . . . The tidal current runs to and fro in its unceasing service, crowded with memories of men and ships it had borne to the rest of home or to the battles of the sea. It had known and served all the men of whom the nation is proud . . .

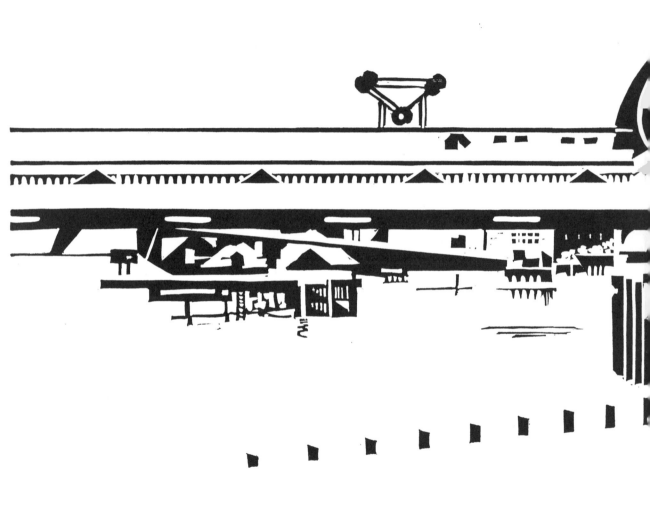

THE DOME

In Xanadu did Kubla Khan
A stately pleasure-dome decree :
Where Alph, the sacred river, ran
Through caverns measureless to man
Down to a sunless sea.
So twice five miles of fertile ground
With walls and towers were girdled round :
And there were gardens bright with sinuous rills,
Where blossomed many an incense-bearing tree ;
And here were forests ancient as the hills,
Enfolding sunny spots of greenery.

The shadow of the dome of pleasure
Floated midway on the waves ;
Where was heard the mingled measure
From the fountain and the caves.
It was a miracle of rare device,
A sunny pleasure-dome with caves of ice!

The modern pleasure park, which is the Dome itself, falls a little short of Coleridge's vision. The original idea was a modern Festival of Britain to mark the new millennium. It was planned by John Major's Conservative government, specifically by Michael Heseltine, and became a popular issue when Tony Blair became Prime Minister in 1997. Many argued that it would be too expensive but he seized upon it as a symbol of the bright new Britain that his government was inaugurating. It will be, he said, 'a triumph of confidence over cynicism, boldness over blandness, excellence over mediocrity'. In fact, the Millennium Night celebration itself and the lack of public support for its contents suggest that he got his epithets the wrong way round: cynicism triumphed over confidence, blandness over boldness, and mediocrity over excellence. Dreams and visions never quite become real:

The Millennium Dome project lost money, and its way, and became a national joke and an embarrassment.

As far as the Dome itself is concerned this is unfair. It is a striking and unmistakable landmark. When it was built it was the world's largest domed structure. (It is not technically a dome at all as it is not self-supporting but is held up by its masts.) The twelve yellow support masts are one hundred metres high and represent the twelve months of the year and the twelve hours on a clock face. Its diameter is three hundred and sixty five metres, one metre for each day of the year, all of which neatly links it to Greenwich and her mean time. As 2000 was a leap year it should have been a little bigger, should perhaps have had a retractable metre. The entire roof structure weighs less than the air it contains and is made of a coated glass fibre fabric, and is fifty metres high in the middle.

The architect was Richard Rogers, the contractors McAlpine, and the engineer Buro Happold.

Those who prefer the past to the present should go from the Dome to Greenwich by way of the foot

THE DOME

tunnel under the Thames. This starts on the Isle of Dogs and was opened in 1902 to provide a securer crossing than the ferries provided. You enter a neat round brick building and take the lift when it's working or stairs when it isn't down about fifteen metres and then walk the 370 metres under the river to emerge near the Cutty Sark. The tunnel has an internal diameter of three metres and is surfaced with glazed tiles. As you walk, think about the weight of water above your head, wonder about the quality of its maintenance, and try not to let your pace quicken.

Claustrophobics might wish to avoid the tunnel and take the Docklands light railway instead. This relatively futuristic line started in 1997 and has trains with no drivers and stations with no staff and serves the redeveloped areas of east London, the places that feature in Dickens and Mayhew.

Either system will bring you to Greenwich, a world heritage site, perhaps the only one in the known universe that includes a museum devoted to ladies fans. Now in the days of smoke control it is one of the pleasantest parts of the city, with a royal park and a cluster of beautiful buildings all set on the slopes of a hill from which there are fine views, including the Dome. Here is perhaps the centre of space and time as it is the home of the Greenwich meridian and of Greenwich mean time. The National Maritime Museum, is the fitting place to keep John Harrison's chronometers. Before Harrison,

ships used dead reckoning. This was often just that, informed guesses as to the position of a ship after a long voyage could too easily lead to shipwreck. Harrison's solution was a clock or watch that would remain reliable despite being a long time at sea, through storm and varying weather. His chronometers are marvels of craftsmanship and also objects of great beauty and worth a pilgrimage. The many ships that sailed out from the great port of London past Greenwich travelled more safely thanks to these small creations.

You can visit most of these buildings, including the Royal Observatory and parts of Greenwich Hospital, one of Wren's finest buildings. It was founded by William III immediately after the death of Queen Mary, his consort, and was intended as an asylum for wounded and disabled sailors, in whom Queen Mary was greatly interested. It housed about three thousand and was closed in 1869. When the Hospital was occupied by the pensioners it became one of the sights of London, and it is possible, says Dickens Junior, that a too liberal distribution of baksheesh on the part of the public may have had something to do with the deterioration which was observable in the manners and customs of the pensioners during the later days of their existence – so tourist nuisance is not a modern phenomenon.

CANARY WHARF

Canary Wharf was for many a symbol of Thatcher's Britain, raising temples to finance, or greed, on a part of London that was once proudly, fiercely, working class, or in the stranglehold of the unions, depending on your point-of-view. The destruction of communities that is necessary for such redevelopment is irreversible, and anonymous uniformity results, but with better bathrooms. When I was working in London in the sixties you could take a boat trip round the docks and imagine yourself with Pip and Magwitch in the great climax to *Great Expectations*, in which the river provides a fitting symbol for what passes irrevocably. The docks have gone and the old warehouses and landing stages on the river are rapidly disappearing and being replaced by modern glass and concrete buildings. Those who mourn the old world's passing should read more of the history of the people who lived and worked there. The best recorder of the past is Henry Mayhew. His great work, *London Labour and the London Poor*, was first published in 1851 and was revised about ten years later. He writes with compassion and an honest eye and often in the words of the poor themselves.

He describes London Dock, an area of ninety acres:

As you enter the dock the sight of the forest of masts in the distance, and the tall chimneys vomiting clouds of black smoke, and the many coloured flags flying in the air, has a most peculiar effect; while the sheds with the monster wheels arching through the roofs look like the paddle-boxes of huge steamers. Along the quay you see, now men with their faces blue with indigo, and now gaugers, with their long brass-tipped rule dripping with spirit from the cask they have been probing. Then will come a group of flaxen haired sailors chattering German; and next a black sailor, with a cotton handkerchief twisted turban-like round his head. Presently a blue smocked butcher, with fresh meat, and a bunch of cabbages in the tray on his shoulder; and shortly afterwards a mate, with green paroquets in a wooden cage. Here you will see sitting on a bench a sorrowful-looking woman, with new bright cooking tins at her feet, telling you she is an emigrant preparing for her voyage. As you pass along this quay the air is pungent with tobacco; on that it overpowers you with the fumes of rum; then you are nearly sickened with the stench of hides, and huge bins of horns; and shortly afterwards the atmosphere is fragrant with coffee and spice. Nearly everywhere you meet stacks of cork, or else yellow bins of sulphur, or lead-coloured copper-ore. As you enter this warehouse, the flooring is sticky, as if it had been newly tarred, with the sugar that has leaked through the casks; and as you descend into the dark vaults, you see long lines of lights hanging from the black arches, and lamps flitting about midway. Here you sniff the fumes of the wine, and there the peculiar fungus-smell of dry rot; then the jumble of sounds as you pass along the dock blends in anything but sweet concord.

overleaf, further views of CANARY WHARF

THE CUTTY SARK

Jerome Fenniman stopped and stared at the blackened hull of the Cutty Sark, her ribs exposed to the morning. There were several other people standing and gazing in silence, as if they were standing round an open grave. He stared but his mind was empty. I'm a poet, he said to himself, and here is something new, something no one has written about before. Here are striking images, endless metaphors waiting to be exploited. 'Exploited', perhaps that was the problem. Lately he had come to see himself as a scavenger, a preyer on other people's misfortunes, a literary ambulance-chaser. Or, to put it more honestly – and what was a poet if not a user of the exact words? – what he was in fact now was an ex-poet.

Though could he even be an ex-poet if he had never published a single poem? Was he not a never-poet? He pulled his notebook out of his pocket, flicked through to a clean page, trying not to read the limp phrases he had written before, and set himself to write. Yet though he tried to capture the smell, the pathos, the sheer incredibility of the wreck before him he found he was constantly thinking how suitable it was, how the Vikings had pulled ships on to the land and set fire to them. How different funerals would be if crematoriums – crematoria? – put your loved one into some kind of boat and burnt them on the grass. Undertakers would have catalogues from small dinghies up. Perhaps someone stinking rich had slipped some dishonest undertaker an enormous bribe.

This was a terrible thought and he looked quickly round, fearing someone had sensed his blasphemy. Nor did he see this turning into a poem anyone would publish. At best he'd have a rejection letter to start to a file. Was he the only poet who was not only unpublished but who had never submitted a single poem for anyone else's judgement? Was it because he still dared not emerge from his obscurity? Was he afraid his poem would be read by someone deep in the Vatican and the hounds of heaven would be set upon him?

He turned his mind back to the remains before him, forced himself to pay proper attention to her, to the sadness of her life. He knew she had only made eight voyages to fetch tea to the nation's tables as the Suez Canal had made her redundant. Her life, so short a time free on the world's waters, so long imprisoned on the land stared at by the idle. My life, thought Jerome, has had just one voyage, and that through the Suez Canal, and I have fetched nothing, done nothing, and drawn no crowds. My origins are obscure, farcical even.

The baby had been left on the steps of the chapel at the mother house of the Brotherhood of St Jerome in North Queensland during Sunday mass. Brother Donald was reading the Gospel, 'If any man compel thee to go one mile, go with him two,' when the baby's imperious wail rose above his rather quiet voice. The brothers made discreet enquiries but could not discover any mother for the child. They feared that one of themselves was the father and that scandal would destroy their dubious authority in the area. We will keep him here, the Superior decided. They called him Jerome after their patron saint, and Fenniman after the words he had chosen to interrupt. He grew up in the mother house, attended the brothers' school, and seemed destined to move smoothly into the order. He took all that happened to him as if he had no will of his own, as if the brothers' vow of obedience had been bred into him.

Then the bishop intervened. 'Jerome needs space, a few months in the outside world, before making a decision like this,' he said. 'He will come to England with me.' And so he dutifully went as unpaid bishop's dogsbody, making no more of a decision in this than in the taking of vows. In the middle of the ocean the Cutty Sark had long ago flown over, wings spread, they came the equator and the bishop went over the side in a Crossing the Line ceremony that got out of hand, perhaps because too many of the sailors had been to catholic schools. Jerome was, for the first time in his life, out of the hands of the church. Other passengers had a collection for him and he landed at Tilbury feeling quite rich, a feeling that lasted about two days. But he survived, kept away from churches and priests, and disappeared into the anonymous city.

Always he had wanted to write. Brother Donald had encouraged him when he had been a child in the school. had praised his writing, pinned it to the classroom wall. He had visions of being like St John of the Cross, a great poet for the Lord, writing in the obscurity of the Australian bush, using the imagery of that strange burnt land. But the bustle and dirty and noise of the great city had confused him. He had writer's block without ever having been a writer.

As he stared at the Cutty Sark and brooded on life in the mother house words came to him and he scribbled them down:

ADAM SPEAKS

I should have said:

Your Eden is a zoo,
us the exhibits for
the cool of your day.
Out here, OK, it's no
paradise, but it is
a whole new world.

I should have said:

The woman gave me
to eat, thank God.

He took a pound coin out of his pocket and dropped it into the box for the restoration appeal. It was the least he could do. The Cutty Sark had let his mind sail free. Now he would go and be a poet.

overleaf THE CUTTY SARK

My favourite chapter in Mayhew's great book, *London Labour and the London Poor,* is on the mudlarks who worked on this part of the river.

There is another class who may be termed river-finders, although their occupation is connected only with the shore; they are commonly known by the name of 'mudlarks', from being compelled, in order to obtain the articles they seek, to wade sometimes up to their middle through the mud left on the shore by the retiring tide. These poor creatures are certainly about the most deplorable in their appearance of any I have met with in the course of my inquiries. They may be seen of all ages, from mere childhood to positive decrepitude, crawling among the barges at the various wharfs along the river; it cannot be said that they are clad in rags, for they are scarcely half covered by the tattered indescribable things that serve them for clothing; their bodies are grimed with the foul soil of the river, and their torn garments stiffened up like boards with dirt of every possible description. Among the mudlarks may be seen many old women, and it is indeed pitiable to behold them, especially during the winter, bent double with age and infirmity, paddling and groping among the wet mud for small pieces of coal, chips of wood, or any sort of refuse washed up by the tide. These women always have with them an old basket or an old tin kettle, in which they put whatever they chance to find. It usually takes them a whole tide to fill this receptacle, but when filled, it is as much as the feeble old creatures are able to carry home.

At one of the stairs in the neighbourhood of the pool, I collected about a dozen of these unfortunate children; there was not one of them over twelve years of age, and many of them were but six. It would be almost impossible to describe the wretched group, so motley was their appearance, so extraordinary their dress, and so stolid and inexpressive their countenances. Some carried baskets, filled with the produce of their morning's work, and other old tin kettles with iron handles. Some, for want of these articles, had old hats filled with the bones and coals they had picked up; and others, more needy still, had actually taken the caps from their own heads, and filled them with what they had happened to find. The muddy slush was dripping from their clothes and utensils, and forming a puddle in which they stood. There did not appear to be among the whole group as many filthy cotton rags to their backs as, when stitched together, would have been sufficient to form the material of one shirt. There were the remnants of one or two jackets among them, but so begrimed and tattered that it would have been difficult to have determined either the original material or make of the garment. On questioning one, he said his father was a coal-backer; he had been dead eight years; the boy was nine years old. His mother was alive; she went out charring and washing when she could get any such work to do. She had 1s. a day when she could get employment, but that was not often; he remembered once to have had a pair of shoes, but it was a long time since. 'It is very cold in winter,' he said, 'to stand in the mud without shoes,' but he did not mind it in the summer. He had been three years mud-larking, and supposed he should remain a mud-lark all his life. What else could he be? for there was nothing else that he knew how to do. Some days he earned a 1d., and some days 4d . . .

The lad of whom I speak was discovered by me now nearly two years ago 'mud-larking' on the banks of the river near the docks. He was a quick intelligent little fellow, and had been at the business, he told me, about three years. He had taken to mud-larking, he said, because his clothes were too bad for him to look for anything better. He worked every day, with 20 or 30 boys, who might all be seen at daybreak with their trousers tucked up, groping about, and picking out the pieces of coal from the mud on the banks of the Thames. He went into the river up to his knees, and in searching the mud he often ran pieces of glass and long nails into his feet. When this was the case, he went home and dressed the wounds, but returned to the riverside directly, 'for should the tide come up,' he added, 'without my having found something, why I must starve till next low tide.' In the very cold weather he and his other shoeless companions used to stand in the hot water that ran down the river side from some of the steam-factories, to warm their frozen feet.

The rest of the histories may easily be imagined, for there was a painful uniformity in the stories of all the children: they were either the children of the very poor, who, by their own improvidence or some overwhelming calamity, had been reduced to the extremity of distress, or else they were orphans, and compelled from utter destitution to seek for the means of appeasing their hunger in the mud of the river. That the majority of this class are ignorant, and without even the rudiments of education, and that many of them from time to time are committed to prison for petty thefts, cannot be wondered at. Nor can it even excite our astonishment that, once within the walls of a prison, and finding how much more comfortable it is than their previous condition, they should return to it repeatedly. As for the females growing up under such circumstances, the worst may be anticipated of them.

The amount of misery the Thames has flowed past over the years is unfathomable. Charles Dickens was never honest enough, could never be honest enough if he wanted the comfortable to read his books, but is credited in the popular mind with stirring up decency. Henry Mayhew's contribution is not remembered enough.

(Note: Using the retail price index, one shilling had the modern purchasing power of about £4, and one old penny would be about equivalent to 34 new pence.)

With the rapid growth of London in the nineteenth century the existing bridges became inadequate for the traffic, a phenomenon we are also familiar with today. This was especially true of London Bridge which could not take the number of carts and pedestrians who needed to cross the river. An ingenious solution was tried first: what can claim to be London's first underground railway. Charles Dickens Jnr wrote in his *Dictionary of the Thames* of 1887:

> Tower Subway. – A curious feat of engineering skill, in the shape of an iron tube seven feet in diameter driven through the bed of the Thames between Great Tower-hill (left bank) and Vine-street (right bank). The original intention was to have passengers drawn backwards and forwards in a small tram omnibus. This, however, was found unremunerative, and, the rails having been taken up, the tunnel has since been open as a footway. Unfortunately, however, after subtracting from its diameter the amount necessary to afford a sufficient width of platform, there is not much headroom left, and it is not advisable for any but the very briefest of Her Majesty's lieges to attempt the passage in high-heeled boots, or with a hat to which he attaches any particular value. It has, however, one admirable quality, that of having cost remarkably little in construction.

An Italian, Edmondo De Amicis, described walking through the Subway in his *Jottings about London* of 1874:

As I was thinking of these things I disappeared from the world indeed, going down a lighted spiral staircase which buries itself in the earth on the right bank of the Thames, opposite the Tower. I went down and down between two dingy walls until I found myself at the round opening of the gigantic iron tube, which seems to undulate like a great intestine in the enormous belly of the river. The inside of this tube presents the appearance of a subterranean corridor, of which the end is invisible. It is lighted by a row of lights as far as you can see, which shed a veiled light, like sepulchral lamps; the atmosphere is foggy; you go along considerable stretches without meeting a soul; the walls sweat like those of an aqueduct; the floor moves under your feet like the deck of a vessel; the steps and voices of the people coming the other way give forth a cavernous sound, and are heard before you see the people, and they at a distance seem like great shadows; there is, in short, a sort of something mysterious, which without alarming causes in your heart a vague sense of disquiet. When then you have reached the middle and no longer see the end in either direction, and feel the silence of a catacomb, and know not how much farther you must go, and reflect that in the water beneath, in the obscure depths of the river, is where suicides meet death, and that over your head vessels are passing, and that if a crack should open in the wall you would not even have the time to recommend your soul to God, in that moment how lovely seems the sun!

TOWER BRIDGE

The opening of Tower Bridge in 1894 meant that people were no longer prepared to pay the half-penny toll and the tunnel soon closed to the public. The new bridge presented a particular problem as it crossed the river at its busiest and ocean-going ships had to reach the wharves. Victorian ingenuity came up with several solutions, including one where carts would be hauled up by hydraulic lifts to a high-level crossing. The design finally selected was the design of Horace Jones, who was responsible for both Billingsgate and Smithfield markets and who was known for completing his projects 'with strict regard to the financial portion of the contract'. He worked with the engineer John Wolfe Barry. Between them they produced what is London's most iconic bridge, and what must be one of the most recognisable bridges in the world.

Its famous design is only partly because of the practical need to allow ships to pass. Because it was being built so close to the Tower of London the city fathers believed that a gothic style was essential to harmonise. Fortunately this idea does not always prevail or we would not now have the marvellous Millennium Bridge leading to St Paul's. The towers are of Portland stone in a Scottish Baronial style. In fact, the actual bridge is made of steel which this stone conceals. Those who spent their childhoods with their Meccano were able to reproduce the actual structure of the bridge quite fairly. Barry himself was modern enough to feel uneasy and in a lecture he said:

. . . some purists will say that the lamp of truth has been sadly neglected in this combination of materials [but I hope] we may forget that the towers have skeletons as much concealed as that of the human body, of which we do not think when we contemplate examples of manly or feminine beauty . . .

which is true but perhaps not the point. Horace Jones died before the bridge was finished and after his death some changes were made to his design, especially to the cladding. He had wanted red brick; the stone came after his death.

The drawbridge gives the bridge a medieval appearance but is one of the wonders of Victorian engineering. The bascules (the roadway sections) weigh one thousand two hundred tons each yet rise by eighty degrees in just one minute. This is achieved because each is a seesaw and so counter-balanced. When the bridge was first opened ships had right of way and could demand passage but this was soon seen to be very impractical and they then had to give a day's notice. They had expected that pedestrians would climb to the higher level if the bridge was open (two hundred and six steps, but there were lifts) but most preferred to stand and stare, especially as the walkways, like those of modern estates, became a place for muggings and prostitution. The bridge is now still opened about one thousand times a year and, with the houses of parliament, is one of the great landmarks of Victorian Gothic.

overleaf TOWER BRIDGE

While the Thames runs through almost all of Dickens it is strangely absent from the work of William Shakespeare. William Blake is a better guide:

> I wander through each chartered street,
> Near where the chartered Thames does flow,
> And mark in every face I meet,
> Marks of weakness, marks of woe.

Geography was not something that interested Shakespeare as he could happily give Bohemia a coast. There are those who seize upon any reference to tides in his writing as references to the ebb and flow of the Thames, but this is to stretch interpretation. In over one hundred and fifty sonnets he never uses the river as an image. The country boy growing up in Warwickshire seems to have the English obsession with the sea; its imagery pervades his writing and is in some of his most memorable lines. Yet he worked in London at a time when the river was the main highway, and his Globe theatre was on its southern bank, about two hundred metres from its modern reconstruction. This building reflects the heritage culture that blights England, the nostalgia for the imaginary Golden Age, John Major's evoking of George Orwell's spinsters cycling to early communion.

And yet . . . The theatre is part of the remarkable regeneration of this part of London and is near Tate Modern, the great and surprising success story. This reused an industrial building, one of the power stations along the river, and turned it into a temple to modern art. It attracts five million visitors a year from a nation whose best-selling tabloids sneer endless at any art that might not be useful for ornamenting boxes of inferior chocolates. Bankside power station was designed by Giles Gilbert Scott and opened in 1947. Its magnificent turbine hall has become the heart of the Tate, not only as a striking space in itself but also as the site for a series of dramatic installations that have managed in a wide variety of different ways to enthral the crowds.

For those who find the art work within the building difficult to appreciate there are the windows over the Thames. You look across to St Paul's, a building I find hard to love, or even like, over the Millennium bridge, which in its beauty matches anything to be found inside the Tate. Yet, like the art, the bridge became an object of universal derision when it first opened to the public before becoming a universal favourite.

The Wobbly Bridge, as it was mockingly called at first, was proposed in 1854 but had to wait until 2000 to open. The competition to design the bridge was won by Norman Foster with Anthony Caro and Ove Arup. The crowds drawn to walk over the bridge caused it to wobble. Albert Bridge was notorious for this, and actually has a notice on it saying that troops crossing must break step. The bridge was closed for almost two years while the 'synchronous lateral excitation' was cured. One of the surprising things about the bridge is that it is a suspension one, though few crossing would guess this.

If only its architects had built a theatre . . .

"But it doesn't wobble!" Charlotte wailed. It was too much: nine red kites and now this dull bridge.

All the way from Oxford to Victoria, with all the other people on the coach there listening, her mother had gone on and on. The worst of it was her using such a baby name, the Wobbly Bridge she kept calling it, as if Charlotte was still exciting by stories of trolls under rickety-rackety bridges. She'd tuned her mother's voice out after a while and stared out of the window, looking for the red kites her father had taught her to recognise. There were more of them now than there had been when he had travelled with them to London and pointed them out. Why couldn't he live with them any more? If she could count ten red kites then he would come back . . .

"I don't think you listened to a word I said," her mother scolded. "Of course it doesn't wobble now. Don't be such a baby!"

"Oh yes, it does," said a man. He had come up to them almost as if he was expecting to meet them there though she had never seen him before. "You need a special kind of magic, Charlotte." And how does he know my name, she wondered but then thought, he's another one treating me like a baby.

"Are you a magician then?" her mother asked, in that fake voice she put on when she was meeting people.

"Yes, I'm the bridge wobbler," he said, quite straight-faced. "Now, Charlotte has to stand between us, facing you. Put your hand on her shoulders. Now I place mine on top of yours just so.

Right, listen very carefully. The magic only works if your eyes are tight shut, absolutely completely shut. And no one must speak. Eyes tight shut. Mouths tight shut. Ready?"

This is so silly, Charlotte thought. It's obvious what will happen. He's going to push me from side to side and pretend it's the bridge wobbling. What she couldn't understand was why her mother was joining in. But unless she made a scene she would just have to let herself be taken for a fool.

"Ready?" the man repeated. Charlotte closed her eyes and nodded her head. The pressure increased on her shoulders and she felt herself being pushed from side to side. Embarrassment flooded her. Suppose someone from school saw her?

At last she could bear it no longer. She opened her eyes. She saw the man kissing – no, eating – her mother, and her whole world rocked.

It is hardly possible to open one of Charles Dicken's novels without finding the river and its bridges. Among the many possible extracts, here is the opening of one of his finest novels, *Our Mutual Friend* (1864):

In these times of ours, though concerning the exact year there is no need to be precise, a boat of dirty and disreputable appearance, with two figures in it, floated on the Thames, between Southwark bridge which is of iron, and London Bridge which is of stone, as an autumn evening was closing in.

The figures in this boat were those of a strong man with ragged grizzled hair and a sun-browned face, and a dark girl of nineteen or twenty, sufficiently like him to be recognizable as his daughter. The girl rowed, pulling a pair of sculls very easily; the man, with the rudder-lines slack in his hands, and his hands loose in his waistband, kept an eager look out. He had no net, hook, or line, and he could not be a fisherman; his boat had no cushion for a sitter, no paint, no inscription, no appliance beyond a rusty boathook and a coil of rope, and he could not be a waterman; his boat was too crazy and too small to take in cargo for delivery, and he could not be a lighterman or river-carrier; there was no clue to what he looked for, but he looked for something, with a most intent and searching gaze. The tide, which had turned an hour before, was running down, and his eyes watched every little race and eddy in its broad sweep, as the boat made slight head-way against it, or drove stern foremost before it, according as he directed his daughter by a movement of his head. She watched his face as earnestly as he watched the river. But, in the intensity of her look there was a touch of dread or horror.

Allied to the bottom of the river rather than the surface, by reason of the slime and ooze with which it was covered, and its sodden state, this boat and the two figures in it obviously were doing something that they often did, and were seeking what they often sought. Half savage as the man showed, with no covering on his matted head, with his brown arms bare to between the elbow and the shoulder, with the loose knot of a looser kerchief lying low on his bare breast in a wilderness of beard and whisker, with such dress as he wore seeming to be made out of the mud that begrimed his boat, still there was a business-like usage in his steady gaze. So with every lithe action of the girl, with every turn of her wrist, perhaps most of all with her look of dread or horror; they were things of usage.

'Keep her out, Lizzie. Tide runs strong here. Keep her well afore the sweep of it.'

Trusting to the girl's skill and making no use of the rudder, he eyed the coming tide with an absorbed attention. So the girl eyed him. But, it happened now, that a slant of light from the setting sun glanced into the bottom of the boat, and, touching a rotten stain there which bore some resemblance to the outline of a muffled human form, coloured it as though with diluted blood. This caught the girl's eye, and she shivered.

'What ails you?' said the man, immediately aware of it, though so intent on the advancing waters; 'I see nothing afloat.'

The red light was gone, the shudder was gone, and his gaze, which had come back to the boat for a moment, travelled away again. Wheresoever the strong tide met with an impediment, his gaze paused for an instant. At every mooring-chain and rope, at every stationery boat or barge that split the current into a broad arrowhead, at the offsets from the piers of Southwark Bridge, at the paddles of the river steamboats as they beat the filthy water, at the floating logs of timber lashed together lying off certain wharves, his shining eyes darted a hungry look. After a darkening hour or so, suddenly the rudder-lines tightened in his hold, and he steered hard towards the Surrey shore.

Always watching his face, the girl instantly answered to the action in her sculling; presently the boat swung round, quivered as from a sudden jerk, and the upper half of the man was stretched out over the stern.

The girl pulled the hood of a cloak she wore, over her head and over her face, and, looking backward so that the front folds of this hood were turned down the river, kept the boat in that direction going before the tide. Until now, the boat had barely held her own, and had hovered about one spot; but now, the banks changed wiftly, and the deepening shadows and the kindling lights of London Bridge were passed, and the tiers of shipping lay on either hand.

Dickens's son describes the bridge here in his *Dictionary of the Thames* of 1887:

Southwark Bridge has of late years been much improved by the introduction of a little colour into the painting of its ironwork arches, which were formerly all in solemn black, and had a very heavy appearance. The credit of being the handsomest iron bridge across the river rests between it and Blackfriars Bridge; and on the whole, though the latter is the more gorgeous, the former is perhaps the more striking. The length is 708 ft or little more than half that of Waterloo. The arches, three in number, rest on stone piers; the centre arch having a span of 402 ft – the longest ever attempted until the adoption of the tubular principle – and the two shore arches 210 ft cables. From the inconvenience of its approaches this handsome bridge has been comparatively valueless from the first .

HUNGERFORD BRIDGE

It was the third Father Christmas that worried her.

She had over the years learnt to look for omens, though other people might think of them as warning signs. It was like the old saying, 'Take what you want, but pay the price.' She believed she could not live without her weekly visit to the Festival Hall, her immersion in music. It carried her through her dull job, her lonely life, the sheer pointlessness of it all. The two hours or so of Beethoven or Brahms, or her new favourite, Janáček – oh the exultation of the 'Glagolitic Mass' that she had heard last week! – made it all worthwhile. And it wasn't just the concert itself. There was the wonderful moment when the new programme appeared among the junk mail, the marking of it with her 2B pencil, the exquisite agony of choosing the one concert each week that she allowed herself, the buying of the tickets – and if she was lucky her favourite woman was behind the window and ready to exchange friendly words – the feel of the cardboard strips in her hands . . .

The price had not been financial. She could afford, just, her weekly seat, her one luxury. It might mean being a little careful about everything else but no, the price she had had to pay had been Hungerford bridge. To come out from a concert, drunk with sound, to face the steps up to the foot-bridge was the path from paradise to hell. The fact that hell was raised up somehow made it worse. The beggars! The hands stretched out to the rich and comfortable who had the money to pay for an evening's entertainment. The curses shouted at those who passed uncaring by. The weekly dilemma: hurry by and be sworn at, or drop in the coins that would pay for her careful lunch next day? But to which beggar? There were too many. It seemed wrong to reward the most foul-mouthed. The drunks! The shouting, singing, vomiting . . . Oh it was all too terrible.

And there was the fear. There were such stories of robberies and violence. There had been those students, beaten and then thrown into the river while their attackers – and one of them a girl! – laughed and joked. Even though she was careful to cross in the crowd spilling out of the concert she was terrified that one night she would somehow be hurrying along that narrow path by herself, with the clattering of the trains covering her cries for help as dark figures raised their arms against her . . .

Even after coming down those steep steps off the bridge there was still the Embankment station, so grubby and depressing, as the gateway into the depths of hell that was the tube.

Yes, she paid a price for the pleasure she took.

HUNGERFORD BRIDGE

She wished she could believe in guardian angels, that someone cared for her, cared about her, but she knew that she was on her own, that no one would care if it was her unconscious body that was heaved over into the dark river while teenagers laughed. Perhaps it was her lack of faith that made her superstitious. As a child, dancing down the road, one hand holding on to her mother, the other on to her father, jumping over the lines between the paving stones was a joke. No one believed that the bears were really round the corner waiting to eat her, but it was wonderful to pretend. Now that the bears were there, really there in human shape, jumping the cracks was shameful and she refused to let her mind admit what she did every week to keep them away.

Then the new bridge opened. That week she allowed herself, for the very first time, a second evening at the Festival Hall. To walk across, especially that first summer, was a pleasure, a rounding off of the evening. The worst she ever met was a gaggle of teenage girls, skirts down to their navels, singing – she supposed it was singing – the Spice Girls' hits. She knew that was what they were singing because a passing woman tutted, in a friendly way and told her.

Then there were the Father Christmases. She had

gone to buy her tickets, her Christmas present to herself, and was walking back over the Golden Jubilee bridge. The first one made her smile, he was so tall and thin. When she saw the second she thought, suppose children see him! How can they believe in Father Christmas if they see two of him? When she saw the third striding towards her she felt worried. Was even this beautiful bridge going to turn nasty?

When the third Father Christmas was near he sang the first line of Silent Night at her. "Oh," she said before she could stop herself, "you have a lovely voice."

"Thank you," he said, and smiled. "Why don't you come to the concert then?"

He was in a choir, it turned out, and for this free Christmas concert in the Festival Hall they were all dressed in Father Christmas robes. She turned and walked with him and sat and drank a cup of tea and enjoyed all the old tunes from her childhood. After it was over she went to find her Father Christmas to thank him. "Give me your name and address," he said, "and I'll put you on our mailing list."

She walked back over the bridge as the lights were coming on. The Bridge of Smiles, she said to herself.

overleaf HUNGERFORD BRIDGE

THE LONDON EYE

Until 2000 the best panoramic view of London was a boat trip on the Thames, but then the Eye opened. It was to have been temporary, part of the millennial celebrations, but it was so successful and so popular that it is now a permanent and well-loved feature of the London skyline, and is the most popular paid-for tourist attraction in Britain with over three and a half million visitors a year. On a clear day you can see for forty kilometres in all directions. The wheel represents the turning of the century and there are thirty-two capsules, one for each London borough.

The official British Airways London Eye web site offers a virtual tour of the Thames. In 1909 H G Wells sent the narrator of *Tono Bungay* down the river in a real, if fictional, boat, replicating almost exactly the path our book takes in reverse about one hundred years later:

> To run down the Thames so is to run one's hand over the pages in the book of England from end to end. One begins in Craven Reach and it is as if one were in the heart of old England. Behind us are Kew and Hampton Court with their memories of Kings and Cardinals, and one runs at first between Fulham's episcopal garden parties and Hurlingham's playground for the sporting instinct of our race. The whole effect is English. There is space, there are old trees and all the best qualities of the homeland in that upper reach. Putney, too, looks Anglican on a dwindling scale. And then for a stretch the newer developments slop over . . .

and there come first squalid stretches of mean homes right and left and then the dingy industrialism of the south side, and on the north bank the polite long front of nice houses, artistic, literary, administrative people's residences, that stretches from Cheyne Walk nearly to Westminster and hides a wilderness of slums. What a long slow crescendo that is, mile after mile, with the houses crowding closer, the multiplying succession of church towers, the architectural moments, the successive bridges, until you come out into the second movement of the piece with Lambeth's old palace under your quarter and the houses of Parliament on your bow! Westminster Bridge is ahead of you then, and through it you flash, and in a moment the round-faced clock tower cranes up to peer at you again and New Scotland Yard squares at you, a fat beef-eater of a policeman disguised miraculously as a Bastille.

For a stretch you have the essential London; you have Charing Cross railway station, heart of the world, and the Embankment on the north side with its new hotels overshadowing its Georgian and Victorian architecture, and mud and great warehouses and factories, chimneys, shot towers, advertisements on the south. The northward skyline grows more intricate and pleasing, and more and more does one thank God for Wren. Somerset House is as picturesque as the civil war, one is reminded again of the original England, one feels in the fretted sky the quality of Restoration Lace.

And then comes Astor's strong box and the lawyers' Inns . . .

And in this reach, too, one first meets the sea-gulls and is reminded of the sea. Blackfriars one takes – just under these two bridges and just between them is the finest bridge moment in the world – and behold, soaring up, hanging in the sky over a rude tumult of warehouses, over a jostling competition of traders, irrelevantly beautiful and altogether remote, Saint Paul's! "Of course!" one says, "Saint Paul's!" It is the very figure of whatever fineness the old Anglican culture achieved, detached, a more dignified and chastened Saint Peter's, colder, greyer, but still ornate; it has never been over thrown, never disavowed, only the tall warehouses and all the roar of traffic have forgotten it, every one has forgotten it; the steamships, the barges, go heedlessly by regardless of it, intricacies of telephone wires and poles cut blackly into its thin mysteries, and presently, when in a moment the traffic permits you and you look round for it, it has dissolved like a cloud into the grey blues of the London sky.

And then the traditional and ostensible England falls from you altogether. The third movement begins, the last great movement in the London symphony, in which the trim scheme of the old order is altogether dwarfed and swallowed up. Comes London Bridge, and the great warehouses tower up about you, waving stupendous cranes, the gulls circle and scream in your ears, large ships lie among their lighters, and one is in the port of the world. Again and again in this book I have written of England as a feudal scheme overtaken by fatty degeneration and stupendous accidents of hypertrophy.

For the last time I must strike that note as the memory of the dear neat little sunlit ancient Tower of London lying away in a gap among the warehouses comes back to me, that little accumulation of buildings so provincially pleasant and dignified, overshadowed by that most typical exploit of modern England, the sham Gothic casings to the ironwork of the Tower Bridge. That Tower Bridge is the very balance and confirmation of Westminster's dull pinnacles and tower. That sham Gothic bridge; in the very gates of our mother of change, the Sea!

But after that one is in a world of accident and nature. For the third part of the panorama of London is beyond all law, order, and precedence; it is the seaport and the sea. One goes down the widening reaches through a monstrous variety of shipping, great steamers, great sailing-ships, trailing the flags of all the world, a monstrous confusion of lighters, witches' conferences of brown-sailed barges, wallowing tugs, a tumultuous crowding and jostling of cranes and spars, and wharves and stores . . .

Westminster Bridge is the subject of one of the most memorised poems in English, William Wordsworth's sonnet of 1802 but it is impossible to stand on the same bridge now and recite it as the bridge has been rebuilt. An earlier writer felt differently on the same bridge. In 1763 Casanova, after causing the death of a young woman, determined to kill himself (I have shortened this extract):

Pondering over my plan with the utmost coolness, I went and bought some balls of lead as large as my pockets would hold, and as heavy as I could bear, to carry to the Tower, where I intended to go on foot. On my way I was strengthened in my purpose by the reflection, that if I continued to live I should be tormented for the remainder of my days by the pale shade of the Charpillon reproaching me as her murderer. I even congratulated myself on being able to carry out my purpose without any effort, and I also felt a secret pride in my courage.

I walked slowly on account of the enormous weight I bore, which would assure me a speedy passage to the bottom of the river.

By Westminster Bridge my good fortune made me meet Sir Edgar, a rich young Englishman, who lived a careless and joyous life. I had made his acquaintance at Lord Pembroke's, and he had dined with me several times. We suited one another, his conversation was agreeable, and we had passed many pleasant hours together. I tried to avoid him, but he saw me, and came up and took me by the arm in a friendly manner.

"Where are you going? Come with me, we shall have a pleasant party."

"My dear friend, you must excuse me; I am in a melancholy mood, and I want to be alone to get over it."

Edgar argued, insisted, and joked till at last I said to myself, "A day longer will not matter, I can do the deed when he leaves me, and I shall only have to bear with life a few hours longer."

When Edgar heard that I had no particular object in crossing the bridge he said that we had better turn back, and I let myself be persuaded; but in half an hour I begged him to take me somewhere where I could wait for him, as I could not bear the weight of the lead any longer. I gave him my word of honour that I would meet him at the 'Canon.'

As soon as I was alone I emptied my pockets, and put the leaden balls into a cupboard. Then I waited in the tavern for the young Englishman, doubtful whether he was doing me a service or an injury . . .

Casanova then left to continue his amorous life on the continent.

When I lived in London in the late sixties I walked every evening down to the river from my flat in Pimlico and admired Battersea power station. Its uncompromising grandeur put the day's irritations into perspective and I returned home relaxed and refreshed. I was not aware at the time of the sad decline it would suffer later, nor of the uproar there had been in 1927 when it was proposed. There was fear for the paintings in the Tate Gallery (ironic that the wildly successful Tate Modern should be born from the shell of another power station) and for the 'noble buildings of London', whose number Battersea soon joined.

In the 1920s the electricity was supplied in a very haphazard way. Small private companies generated for particular industries and sold any surplus to the public supply. It was an expensive and chaotic system. The London Power Company was set up in 1925, it seems as a way of staving off the public ownership which was coming to be seen as the only sensible solution. They determined to generate in a few large power stations: Battersea was the first of these. Sir Giles Gilbert Scott was chosen to design the building, and Londoners can be thankful that it did not turn out to be another Liverpool Cathedral but more akin to his red telephone box.

The building has a steel girder frame with brick cladding and is the largest brick building in Europe. It had an Art Deco control room, Italian marble in the turbine room, wrought iron staircases and polished parquet floors. What I also did not know,

in my daily admiration of the building, was that the much-loved silhouette of the four chimneys dates back only to 1953. Gilbert-Scott's building looked long rather than squareish and had one chimney at each end. In 1939 in a survey in The Architects' Journal it was came second in a list of favourite buildings.

The need for more power after the eventual nationalisation of the industry in 1948 led to the construction of Battersea B which produced the building we now have. It was the most efficient of power stations and provided one fifth of London's electricity, with twenty-eight other stations needed to supply the rest.

In 1975 Battersea A closed down and there were rumours that B was to close too. A campaign started to preserve the building and Michael Heseltine awarded it Grade 2 status. It is a sad reflection on British taste that this magnificent building's future appears clouded in doubt and lost in financial fogs.

I was equally familiar with the railway bridge that spans the Thames here, taking trains from Victoria to the south. Yet I never knew that it was called Grosvenor Bridge after England's richest landlord, the Duke of Westminster. Originally the trains came into what was called Pimlico station; a curious name as it was on the south bank of the river, which was relatively inaccessible. Three railway companies combined to build this, the first railway bridge to cross the Thames into central London. It took just one year to build with the first trains crossing on the 9th June 1860, and on two different gauges of track.

The bridge, and Victoria Station, were designed by Sir John Fowler who, with his partner Benjamin Baker, designed the more satisfying Forth Railway Bridge, and later the world's first deep-level underground railway, the Metropolitan. For this he tried to create a fire-less engine by using heated bricks instead of a coal fire but the one prototype built, called Fowler's Ghost, was not a success.

The bridge expanded, until it became three crossings side by side. When in 1963 it had deteriorated too much and had to be replaced this lessened the disruption. It is now a steel bridge with the original piles encased in concrete. It is, in effect ten separate bridges joined together over the four steel spans.

Victoria is not one of the most beautiful of railway stations and the journey south, once past the Thames and the power station, is one of the most depressing routes out of London, which is not a city know for its beautiful approaches. It is perhaps suitable that visiting royalty make their entrance here.

Near the bridge is the tower of the Western Pumping Station. When Joseph Bazalgette designed his sewer system he used gravity to transfer the waste matter from west to east. This meant that by the time it had reached the East End, where it was going to be discharged into the tidal Thames, it was over thirteen metres below the surface. To bring the sewage of London back up he built four steam-powered pumping stations, and this is his Pimlico one.

Charles Dickens Jnr wrote of Battersea Park:

No park or garden in London can compare with the sub-tropical garden. It is emphatically one of the sights which no visitor should fail to see, especially in the latter part of the summer . . . There is every accommodation for cricketers, and boating may be indulged in on the lake, which adds greatly to the picturesqueness of the ingeniously planned grounds.

My affection for this stretch of the Thames reminds me of Ruskin's fine words on Turner:

. . . he attaches himself with the faithfullest child-love to everything that bears an image of the place he was born in. No matter how ugly it is, – has it anything like Maiden Lane, or like Thames' shore? If so, it shall be painted for their sake. Hence, to the very close of life, Turner could endure ugliness which no one else, of the same sensibility, would have borne with for an instant. Dead brick walls, blank square windows, old clothes, market-womanly types of humanity – anything fishy and muddy, like Billingsgate or Hungerford Market, had a great attraction for him; black barges, patched sails, and every possible condition of fog.

ALBERT BRIDGE AND BATTERSEA PARK

Battersea Park is one of the secret treasures of London, known to locals but not to the tourist hordes trailing round the usual sights. Here can be seen Henry Moore's 'Three Standing Figures' and Barbara Hepworth's 'Single Form'. There is also a superior war memorial sculpture, by Eric Kennington, and an entertaining 'Brown Dog' by Nicola Hicks. Perhaps even more admirably, the park usually hosts a student work on show for a year. Add to this playing areas for a variety of sports and games, children's playgrounds and a zoo, and bicycles for hire, with an exhibition space, and music in the bandstand and the cafe – all set within gardens with a lake and you begin to have something Coleridge might have recognised as a Pleasure Ground.

Albert Bridge was much loved by two of our great, but very different, poets. William Blake lived near here and loved the bridge and John Betjeman led the campaign in the nineteen fifties against the old LCC's plans to demolish and rebuild it.

The bridge is named for Prince Albert as he suggested building it. It opened in 1873 and had a method of construction, using cable-stayed rods, that was far ahead of its time. It became, inevitably, too narrow and too fragile for modern traffic but it is now a Grade II listed building with a beautiful colour scheme and prize-winning lighting. As it can claim to be the poet's bridge Robert Herrick's 'Farewell to the Thames' of 1648 would be a suitable reading for both bridge and gardens:

His Teares to Thamasis.

I send, I send here my supremest kiss
To thee my *silver-footed Thamasis.*
No more shall I reiterate thy Strand,
Whereon so many Stately Structures stand:
Nor in the summers sweeter evenings go,
To bath in thee (as thousand others doe.)
No more shall I a long thy christall glide,
In Barge (with boughes and rushes beautifi'd)
With soft-smooth Virgins (for our chast disport)
To *Richmond, Kingstone,* and to *Hampton-Court*:
Never againe shall I with Finnie-Ore
Put from, or draw unto the faithfull shore:
And Landing here, or safely Landing there,
Make way to my *Beloved Westminster:*
Or to the *Golden-cheap-side*, where the earth
Of *Julia Herrick* gave to me my Birth.
May all clean *Nimphs* and curious water Dames,
With Swan-like-state, flote up & down thy streams:
No drought upon thy wanton waters fall
To make them Leane, and languishing at all.
No ruffling winds come hither to discease
Thy pure, and *Silver-wristed Naides.*
Keep up your state ye streams; and as ye spring,
Never make sick your Banks by surfeiting.
Grow young with Tydes, and though I see ye never,
Receive this vow, *so fare-ye-well for ever.*

Battersea is a suitable place to pay homage to Ruskin's enemy, James McNeil Whistler. There is a rather stolid statue to him standing on Cheyne Walk. His Nocturnes are among the most beautiful pictures of the Thames ever painted, thanks to pollution. Claude Monet loved the deadly fogs too and laboured to put their ethereal quality on to his canvases.

At the end of the nineteenth century about eighteen million tons of coal were being burnt in London every year, which spewed two hundred tons of fine soot into the air every day. Ruskin saw in this a symbol of the low standards of morality in the city. One critic of Whistler's Nocturnes, Sydney Colvin, Slade Professor of Art at Cambridge, saw in their '. . . indefinable atmosphere above the houses, half duskiness, half glare . . . the effluence of the city's life'. A terrible beauty was born from the cause of so much, so very much, human sickness and death.

Whistler painted 'Grey and Silver, Old Battersea Bridge, 1863' while he was living in Chelsea across the river from factory chimneys that not only filled the sky with smoke but also the air with their smells, not just of gas and coal but of vinegar, malt, and phosphorus. Baudelaire argued that there is a connection between sound, colour, and perfume and while Whistler was facing the stink and colours across the river his musical background seems to have led him to want to copy the composer's detachment from realistic reproduction. His adoption of the musical term 'nocturne' plainly signalled his intention as clearly as 'impression' did before.

His practice was to be rowed on the river (by Turner's old boatman) until he saw something that interested him. He would then memorise the view and return to his studio and paint on a canvas lying on the floor using very dilute oil paints.

To compare Whistler's painting with, for example, Dickens' poem to fog that opens *Bleak House* (1852) makes you consider the morality of turning such horror into such beauty.

The history of the bridge between Fulham and Putney is perhaps the most interesting of any of the crossings of the tidal Thames. The old London Bridge of nursery rhyme fame was for several hundred years the only bridge across the tidal river with Kingston, above the tide, as the next up stream. Elsewhere ferries had to be used, with their usual problems of safety in the days before regulation.

Fulham became famous for bishops and pots. The bishop of London had his palace here and in 1670 Fulham Pottery, founded by John Dwight, made salt-glazed pots, the first to do so. The village became a favourite place for the rich to build their summer houses away from the stink and disease of the city. The bishop travelled by barge to his job in London, and had the rights for the ferry across to Putney. This became very busy and, as so often in the history of transport, became a bottleneck. During the Civil War the King controlled Kingston Bridge and the Earl of Essex (it's a curious light on the English Revolution that the people's troops were commanded by an earl) wanted to attack from the south. Crossing his army by the ferry was not very practical so he had a 'bridge' constructed in the same way as the annual plague bridge is build across the Guidecca in Venice, with boats tied together. In fact the threat was enough and once the bridge was finished the Royalists went back to Oxford.

Soon after the Restoration a bill was introduced into Parliament in 1671 to allow for the building of a permanent crossing here. The doom-mongers climbed on their hobby horses and rode off in all directions prophesying disasters. One said that Fulham and Putney would become so prosperous that the City of London would fall into ruin. Another claimed that the bridge would succeed where Canute had failed and stop the tide and so destroy the Thames, which would lead to the ruin of the port of London and so in the next war there would be no experienced watermen able to man our warships which would lead to the downfall of the whole country. Yet another went into further flights of fancy and said that, if this was allowed, bridges would spring up all over, even in places like Westminster and Blackfriars. He even threatened to introduce a bill for bridges at Chelsea and Hammersmith. His eloquence won applause and the defeat of the bill.

It was another fifty years before there was another serious attempt to bridge the river here and it was led by the Prime Minister, Sir Robert Walpole. He had been to see the king at Kingston and was riding back to London for a debate in the Commons. When he reach the crossing the ferry was on the north bank of the river and the ferrymen were drinking in the inn there. However much he shouted he was unable to get them to come and carry him across and he had to take the long way round. In 1726 he helped to pass an act for the building of a bridge. He did not hold a grudge against the ferrymen as he made sure they were offered jobs in the customs house when the bridge was built.

PUTNEY BRIDGE

The financing of the project is interesting in a democratic country. To raise money thirty shares in the company were sold at one thousand pounds each, a huge sum then. This gave the shareholders two benefits. They were to receive tolls 'in perpetuity' and they were allowed to vote in elections in both Surrey and Middlesex. Such was the hunger for the vote then that the shares were soon sold off in fractions. A wooden bridge was constructed with a wide central arch for boats to pass under. The construction of the bridge itself took only half the money that was spent; compensation swallowed the rest and the income from tolls was reduced by allowing not only the bishop himself but all the members of his household to cross without paying. Anyone with sufficient confidence would just shout 'Bishop!' and walk across without paying. The king paid a flat fee of £100 a year for all the crossings by his household.

This royal payment links us to another significant date: the introduction in 1752 of the Gregorian calendar. To bring the official date back into line with the seasons, eleven days were dropped from the calendar: everything between September 3rd and 14th. (How many children missed out on their birthday presents that year?) The king made his payment £1.10.00 less that year. His example was followed next spring by the City bankers. They had always paid their taxes to the crown on Lady Day, March 25th, but they added on the eleven days and paid them on April 5th, which is now, illogically, the start of the financial year.

It was from this bridge that Mary Wollstonecraft threw herself in 1795 when she discovered her betrayal by her partner Gilbert Imlay. Virginia Woolf movingly described this splendid woman, and in a dreadful foreshadowing of her own suicide wrote:

> True to her own creed of decisive action, Mary at once soaked her skirts so that she might sink unfailingly, and threw herself from Putney Bridge. But she was rescued; after unspeakable agony she recovered, and then her 'unconquerable greatness of mind', her girlish creed of independence, asserted itself again, and she determined to make another bid for happiness and to earn her living without taking a penny from Imlay for herself or their child.

and she then married William Godwin and died after giving birth to Mary Shelley. Some read her description of the bringing of life to the monster by Frankenstein as inspired by the artificial respiration given to her mother. It is thanks to the competence of some passing watermen that the monster exists at all.

Sir Joseph Bazalgette wrote a damning report on the condition of the wooden bridge in 1880 and was then given the job of designing its replacement, now called Putney Bridge, which was opened in 1886. His bridge here makes an interesting contrast with his Hammersmith bridge.

William Morris wrote unkindly of the new Hammersmith Bridge in *News from Nowhere* in 1891:

> As he formed the words, the train stopped at his station, five minutes' walk from his own house, which stood on the banks of the Thames, a little way above an ugly suspension bridge. He went out of the station, still discontented and unhappy, muttering "If I could but see it! if I could but see it!" but had not gone many steps toward the river before (says our friend who tells the story) all that discontent and trouble seemed to slip off him.
>
> It was a beautiful night of early winter, the air just sharp enough to be refreshing after the hot room and the stinking railway carriage. The wind, which had lately turned a point or two north of west, had blown the sky clear of all cloud save a light fleck of two which went swiftly down the heavens. There was a young moon halfway up the sky, and as the home-farer caught sight of it, tangled in the branches of a tall old elm, he could scarce bring to his mind the shabby London suburb where he was, and he felt as if he were in a pleasant country place – pleasanter, indeed, than the deep country was as he had known it.
>
> He came right down to the riverside, and lingered a little, looking over the low wall to note the moonlit river, near upon high water, go swirling and glittering up to Chiswick Eyot; as for the ugly bridge below, he did not notice it or think of it, except when for a moment (says our friend) it stuck him that he missed the row of lights downstream.

Morris, so good on politics but so limited in his taste, was unable to appreciate the beauty of a modern structure. Today, one hopes, he would be impressed by the lights of the bridge reflecting on the river below. Twice he turned his back on the bridge as he rowed the one hundred and thirty miles from his home in Hammersmith to Kelmscott Manor in Oxfordshire.

Perhaps, though, Morris was prescient for it was from Hammersmith Bridge that T J Cobden-Sanderson threw the type of the Doves Press. He had been the partner of Emery Walker who had become a friend of Morris through their shared interest in printing, and of him Morris said that he 'did not think the day complete without a sight' of Walker. In 1900 Walker and Cobden-Sanderson, a noted book-binder, set up the Doves Press. The clarity and elegance of their books was not matched by their relationship. There are differing accounts of how the type came to be thrown off the bridge, from religious mania through a dispute over design, to a symbolic act when the press closed in 1916. I like the thought that as the letters fell through the murky Thames water they arranged themselves into a final text which lies there patiently waiting for its reader.

One hundred years before the first bridge there was talk of the need for it. Daniel Defoe, in his *Tour through the Whole Island of Great Britain* in 1724, wrote:

Some talk also of building a fine stone bridge over the Thames; but these things are as yet but in embryo, tho' it is not unlikely but they may both be accomplished in time, and also Hammersmith and Chiswick joining thus, would in time be a city indeed.

He did not foresee that Hammersmith, then a major supplier of fruit and vegetables to the hungry mouths of London, would itself be swallowed up by the greater to be absorbed into London itself.

The bridge was opened in 1887 and is 700 feet (213 metres) long and 43 feet (13 metres) wide. It stands on the piers of the first bridge to be built here, in 1824, which was when built the world's longest suspension bridge. The original bridge was not strong enough to take the traffic it attracted, was too narrow, and too low. Punch exaggerated a little in 1842:

> A vessel passing under the bridge is compelled to lower its chimney onto the heads or into the laps of the passengers, besides rendering it incumbent on all on board to bend to circumstances by placing their heads between their knees during the time occupied in passing under the elegant commodious structure.

The new bridge was one of those designed by Sir Joseph Bazalgette who more famously virtually eliminated cholera from London with his sewers. While his sewers are out of sight and mainly out of mind his bridges and embankments form a visible memorial to him. But, like the sewers, his Hammersmith bridge did not foresee the vastly greater flow that constantly threatens to choke it. In fact, it was nearly closed to cars after repairs in 1999 but a local vote allowed then across again.

The bridge became a major feature in that strangest of sporting events, the Boat Race, with the television cameras lingering on the crowds spanning the river. The first bridge opened two years before the first race. There is a popular painting in Tate Britain, 'Hammersmith Bridge on Boat-race Day', which was painted by Walter Greaves when he was just sixteen, probably of the 1862 race, showing crowds hanging from every possible piece of the bridge. It is perhaps the boat race publicity that has led to three attempts to blow it up, in 1939, 1996, and 2000. The first attempt failed when Maurice Childs spotted a smoking suitcase, opened it, saw a bomb, and threw the case in the river, and watched the sixty-foot high column of water it produced. The second bomb failed to go off. The third made a hole in a girder but most of the subsequent disruption was caused by incompetent repairs.

The bridge has been so overtaken by traffic volumes that it has become a daily problem, yet the affection with which it is held has so far preserved it from the vandals who believe in the divine right of the motor car.

Hammersmith Bridge

They were to meet in the middle of the bridge. It had started as a joke. When he had asked her to come for a drink with him at Helen's party she had said, 'But I have a partner.' When he persisted, and as the wine worked in her, she had laughed and said, 'Well, I'll meet you half way,' meaning it metaphorically. At least, she supposed she'd meant it that way, though she wasn't sure, when sober, what it would have meant. She had given him her postcode and work email address, thinking that she would hear no more.

The email came next day: *put p'codes into g-map. guess what – we meet in the middle of chiswick bridge. 6.30 for a drink?* The symbolism was too good for her to resist and she replied with just *ok just one quick one.*

It became their place and time. Something superstitious made her refuse to meet anywhere else even though it wasn't the easiest place for her to get to and she often arrived out of breath and in a panic that she would be too late. Like Cinderella, she thought the exact time had something magic about it. Six thirty five would see her in rags next to a pumpkin. It was, she knew, her way of shutting guilt out of her mind.

As the days shortened it became both harder and easier. Sitting on the bus she felt exposed and tried not to be by a window but once she had got off, and looked round to check no one she knew was watching her, she walked briskly along, her face turned from the people in cars towards the river. On the bridge worry slipped away from her. The lights sparkled in the water, the buildings of the city smiled brightly, and suddenly, waiting in the middle, she felt happy. She began to recognise faces week by week as people passed her in their own private routines. She started leaving work earlier, making excuses, to enjoy that moment when the river carried all away and left her feeling anything was possible.

When she was early she made up stories about the people who passed her, giving them names, lives, families; turning them into characters in a novel. She made up connections between them, found reasons for them to be crossing the bridge that went beyond the mundane hurrying home at the end of the working day. She wove herself into the stories too, giving herself a life she might have had if one choice had been different in the past.

The affair ended, inevitably, next spring and she was careful not to go near the bridge, would go a long way round to avoid it. She had dreams in which somehow she seemed to be the Lady of Shalott floating under the bridge while people leant out of bus windows, laughing. She became pale, edgy.

In July they went to the south of France and there she felt better, regained her balance. She enjoyed the meals she hadn't cooked, sat on the beach at Aiguebelle making up stories about the people, familiar from day to day. On Sunday they went, as they always did, to the L'Annonciade gallery at St-Tropez. She hurried through the temporary exhibition and went upstairs to see what they had hung this year. She was pleased to find old favourites still there and stared for ages at Bonnard's painting of the woman in the bath and thought, how sensible! The Lady in her boat floating on the water seemed just hysterical compared with the serenity of this domestic contentment, and this was so very much a better picture than that Pre-Raphaelite shiny realism. She bought a postcard to put on the fridge door at home.

Life settled back into its comfortable routines. When she allowed herself to think of those months she saw them as a dream, as something unreal that perhaps had never happened. But she avoided the bridge.

One day in winter she had been to a meeting in another part of London and was going home on a bus when she looked up from her book and saw where she was. She pushed her way off and stepped down at the familiar bus stop. She found herself looking anxiously round, but then shook her head. What was she doing wrong? There was no reason why she shouldn't walk on the bridge, have a breath of air, look at the river, no reason at all.

She crossed at the lights so that she would be on the opposite side; something stopped her from walking in her own footsteps to that rendezvous. The view was different here, downstream instead of up, and unfamiliar faces streamed towards her hurrying home. She leant on the parapet, watching the boats.

As she turned to go home she saw him. He was moving along the opposite pavement in that slightly exaggerated hurrying that she had come to know so well. Opposite a woman was standing, as she had stood last year but a little further back, arms raised ready to embrace.

'Half way!' she heard him shout. 'I'll meet you half way.'

She smiled bitterly and turned for home. She was no Lady of Shalott. She would go and have a long soak in a hot bath. She left the bridge, light-hearted.

She smiled and turned for home. This was an old stale story whose ending she knew already. There was nothing here to interest her, nothing to pain her. She was no Lady of Shalott. The river could flow along, knights could come out on the wharves, but she would not be there to be pitied. She would go and have a long soak in a hot bath. She left the bridge, light-hearted.

Kew has two claims to fame, the Royal Botanic Gardens and the rhyme:

> I am his Highness' dog at Kew,
> Pray tell me, Sir, whose dog are you?

which is one of Alexander Pope's more appealing poems. There are also two bridges. The railway bridge was opened in 1869 while the current road bridge of 1903 is the third to have been built on the site and so is not the actual bridge that Oliver Twist crossed on his way to burgle the Maylies, nor that that features in *Three Men in a Boat* when George had an outing in an eight.

Kew, like Brighton, grew in fashion and size because of royal patronage. Prince Frederick, eldest son of King George II had a house in what is now the Gardens, and was an enthusiastic gardener. Frederick's son heard the news of his grandfather's death while he was riding across the bridge at Kew. Horace Walpole wrote:

> Without surprise or emotion, without dropping a word that indicated what had happened. he said his horse was lame and turned back to Kew. At dismounting, he said to the groom, 'I have said this horse is lame; I forbid you to say to the contrary.'

and so he became King George III. George as Prince of Wales opened the first Kew bridge, made of brick, stone and wood, in 1759, in which year Kew Gardens also opened. Thirty years later, in 1789, he opened the new stone bridge.

George came to hate Kew and Fanny Burney describes how his courtiers argued about who would be responsible for moving him there for the sake of his health in one of his bouts of insanity towards the end of 1788.

As the King began to recover Fanny had an alarming experience as she wrote in a letter in February next year (which I have shortened):

> This morning I begged to know where I might walk in safety? In Kew Garden, he said, as the King would be in Richmond. Taking, therefore, the time I had most at command, I strolled into the Garden; I had proceeded nearly half the round, when I suddenly thought I saw the Person of his Majesty! Alarmed past all possible expression, I waited not to know more, but turning back, ran off with all my might – But what was my terror to hear myself pursued! – to hear the voice of the King himself, loudly and hoarsely calling after me 'Miss Burney! Miss Burney!' – I protest I was ready to die; – I knew not in what state he might be at the time; I only knew the orders to keep out of his way were universal; that the Queen would highly disapprove any unauthorised meeting, and that the very action of my running away might deeply, in his present irritable state, offend him.
>
> Nevertheless, on I ran, – too terrified to stop, and in search of some short passage, for the

Garden is full of little labyrinths, by which I might escape. The steps still pursued me, and still the poor hoarse and altered voice rang in my Ears: – more and more foot steps resounded frightfully behind me, – the attendants all running, to catch their eager master, and the voices of the two Doctor Willis's loudly exhorting him not to heat himself so unmercifully.

Heavens how I ran! – and such was my speed, so almost incredible to relate, or recollect, that I fairly believe no one of the whole party could have overtaken me, if these words, from one of the Attendants, had not reached me 'Dr Willis begs you to stop!' – 'I cannot! – I cannot!' – 'I answered, still flying on, – when he called out 'You must, ma'am, it hurts the King to run. –' Then, indeed, I stopt! – in a state of fear really amounting to agony! – I turned round, – I saw the two Doctors had got the King between them, and about 8 Attendants of Dr Willis's were hovering about. As they approached, some little presence of mind happily came to my command; it occurred to me that, to appease the wrath of my flight, I must now shew some confidence; I therefore faced them as undauntedly as I was able.

When they were within a few yards of me, the King called out 'Why did you run away?' – Shocked at a question impossible to answer, yet a little assured by the mild tone of his voice, I instantly forced myself forward, to meet him though the internal sensation which satisfied me this was a step the most proper, to appease his suspicions and displeasure, was so violently combated by the tremor of my nerves, that I fairly think I may reckon it the greatest effort of personal courage I have ever made. I looked up, and met all his wonted benignity of Countenance, though something still of wildness in his Eyes. Think, however, of my surprise, to feel him put both his Hands round my two shoulders, and then kiss my Cheek!

What a Conversation followed! – when he saw me fearless, he grew more and more alive, and made me walk close by his side, away from the Attendants, and even the Willis's themselves, who, to indulge him, retreated. I own myself not completely composed, but alarm I could entertain no more. Every thing that came uppermost in his mind he mentioned; he seemed to have just such remains of his flightiness, as heated his imagination, without deranging his Reason, and robbed him of all control over his speech, though nearly in his perfect state of mind as to his opinions. What did he not say! – He opened his whole Heart to me, – expounded all his sentiments, and acquainted me with all his intentions.

Spare a thought in Kew for the poor tormented monarch.

Teddington lock is the dividing point between the tidal and non-tidal Thames. John Griffith's picture shows what looks suspiciously like three men in a boat (to say nothing of the dog) looking as if they are about to be swamped. This is an incident that ought to be in the book, but, to the lesser happiness of the nation, is not. Two of the three started at Kingston, after coming from London by train, after bribing the driver of the Exeter mail to take them there. They were thus safely above the lock, and heading upstream to Oxford, which was the furthest they reached before turning for home again. It remains one of the funniest of English books with occasional serious passages. Here is Jerome on Moulsey lock, a passage relevant to our picture, if not strictly to our stretch of the river:

> It took us some time to pass through, as we were the only boat, and it is a big lock. I don't think I ever remember to have seen Moulsey lock, before, with only one boat in it. It is, I suppose, Boulter's not even excepted, the busiest lock on the river.
>
> I have stood and watched it sometimes, when you could not see any water at all, but only a brilliant tangle of bright blazers, and gay caps, and saucy hats, and many-coloured parasols, and silken rugs, and cloaks, and streaming ribbons, and dainty whites; when looking down into the lock from the quay, you might fancy it was a huge box into which flowers of every hue and shade had been thrown pell-mell, and lay piled up in a rainbow heap, that covered every corner.
>
> On a fine Sunday it presents this appearance nearly all day long, while, up the stream, and down the stream, lie, waiting their turn, outside the gates, long lines of still more boats; and boats are drawing near and passing away, so that the sunny river, from the Palace up to Hampton Church, is dotted and decked with yellow, and blue, and orange, and white, and red, and pink. All the inhabitants of Hampton and Moulsey dress themselves up in boating costume, and come and mouch round the lock with their dogs, and flirt, and smoke, and watch the boats, and altogether, what with the caps and jackets of the men, the pretty coloured dresses of the women, the excited dogs, the moving boats, the white sails, the pleasant landscape, and the sparkling water, it is one of the gayest sights I know of near this dull old London town.

This is the sunny side of the lock, and a world of innocent pleasures. On the 20th of March 1818 it was rather different, as the lock keeper related:

> . . . It has always been customary with me to rise at dawn of day, because in general ye barges move from Richmond then, & often do before if the moon shines till day. & this was the case on ye 20th early. I rose at just past 4 & was employed in

the office arranging some small matters before ye craft came, when I heard a man's voice calling. I open'd one of the shutters & saw a man standing about half way between my window & the lower gate, and he pointed with his hand and said "Here's a Trow coming". I had no doubt in my own mind but that the Trow was very near, & as the wind blew hard & right into the pound it was highly necessary the gates should be opened & ready. I now took my hat & was going out but the inst I open'd the door a stout fellow rushed in & seized me by the throat. While we were struggling in came 2 more & one of them had something in his hand resembling a sack. I was thrown with violence over a chair and we both came rolling to ye ground & then I felt one of them cover my head & press it so close down that I really began to fear they meant to suffocate me. They soon succeeded in getting the cloth close on my head again. The 3rd man that I heard busy opening ye desks & ye cupboard in which I deposit my change called out to the men that held me "If the old buggar won't be quiet stick it into him" . . . I now began to argue a little, with a mouth almost full of blood, with the man that held me, that if they were men not savages they would not ill treat one old man.

At this Inst. I heard Mrs. S. step from her bed on the floor over our heads and one said "Tom go and see who that is moving about up stairs", but I said "It's only my old dame".

They then took my keys from my coat pocket by rolling me over, and having broke every lock and emptied every small box of Mrs. S. in the other room they all ran out leaving me locked in & in darkness. By their bad discourse I must think them bargemen of lowest class.

I had about 11 or 12 single pound notes & full six pounds silver and ye most part sml silver & 4 or 5 shillings in copper. I do indeed much fear that this is only ye beginning, for which ever lock receives much value it will be a temptation to such villians to make an attempt at ye end of ye week ...

Rich Savory

Teddington is the largest lock on the Thames, and is really three locks, with the largest of them having gates halfway along so that it is used flexibly. The building of the locks started in 1810, and then they were largely rebuilt in 1858, when the narrow skiff lock, humorously called The Coffin, was added. The barge lock was built in 1904. This is 650 feet long and fifty feet wide. The fall, the difference in height of the water above and below the lock, is eight feet ten inches.

There is a neat symbolism in ending our journey up the Thames facing the gates of Teddington lock. The non-tidal river above, though never to be taken for granted as it delights in flooding, is somehow more civilised. The moon no longer pulls it restlessly too and fro; it truly 'glideth at his own sweet will'.

NOTES ON THE ILLUSTRATIONS